In the 1980s plain county boundary signs with the coat of arms began to be replaced with more informative signs proclaiming the county's attractions.

Road Signs

Stuart Hands

A Shire book
in association with the Michael Sedgwick Trust

CONTENTS

This work is published with the assistance of the Michael Sedgwick Trust. Founded in memory of the famous motoring researcher and author Michael Sedgwick (1926–83), the Trust is a Registered Charity to encourage the publishing of new research and recording of motoring history. Suggestions for future projects or donations should be sent to the Hon. Sec. of the Michael Sedgwick Trust, c/o the National Motor Museum, Beaulieu, Hampshire SO42 7ZN, England.

Cover: *A selection of road signs.*

ACKNOWLEDGEMENTS

Thanks are due to Rodney Marshall, Rob Mabbett, Helen Philp, Pauline Sharp and Steve Fenn, and to Lancashire County Council for the photograph on page 13 (top) and B. Barton (ICE/PHEW) for the photograph on page 29 (top right).

British Library Cataloguing in Publication Data: Hands, Stuart. Road Signs. – (A Shire album; 402) 1. Traffic signs and signals – Great Britain – History 2. Street signs – Great Britain – History I. Title II. Michael Sedgwick Trust 388.3′122′0941 ISBN 0 7478 0531 8.

Editorial Consultant: Michael E. Ware, former Director of the National Motor Museum, Beaulieu.

Published in 2005 by Shire Publications Ltd, Cromwell House, Church Street, Princes Risborough, Buckinghamshire HP27 9AA, UK. Website: www.shirebooks.co.uk
Copyright © 2002 by Stuart Hands. First published 2002; reprinted 2005. Shire Album 402. ISBN-10: 0 7478 0531 8; ISBN-13: 978 0 7478 0531 8.
Stuart Hands is hereby identified as the author of this work in accordance with Section 77 of the Copyright, Designs and Patents Act 1988.

Printed in Great Britain by CIT Printing Services Ltd, Press Buildings, Merlins Bridge, Haverfordwest, Pembrokeshire SA61 1XF.

A quintessential English rural scene. This is Braunston in Rutland. The fingerpost enhances rather than detracts. If only the same could be said of the clutter of signs so often seen.

BEGINNINGS

This book is about humble British road signs, legally known as traffic signs, particularly those of the motoring age. I call them 'humble' because they have never attracted the interest of enthusiasts in the manner that railway signs have. They are simply functional, ubiquitous artefacts that are encountered every day and, being commonplace, are rarely viewed in any other way than that for which they are designed. Yet, as one would expect, they reflect the development of road travel in Britain, particularly during the twentieth century.

A complaint often heard is that we now have too much signage on our highways – a situation that is not improved by the proliferation of brown tourist signs. None the less, there is much of interest to observe on the British highway today. It is surprising how many signs of the past still await the observant motorist; it is hoped that this book will enhance the enjoyment brought by these signs.

Section 64 of the Road Traffic Regulation Act 1984 gives the following definition of a traffic sign:

> any object or device (whether fixed or portable) for conveying, to traffic on roads or any specified class of traffic, warnings, information, requirements, restrictions or prohibitions of any description –
>> (a) specified by regulations made by the Ministers acting jointly, or
>> (b) authorised by the Secretary of State,
> and any line or mark on a road for so conveying such warnings, information, requirements, restrictions or prohibitions.

Except in passing, this book does not deal with portable signs or with road markings.

For centuries, signs have been erected to help travellers find their way. The various old crosses found in places like Dartmoor and the North Yorkshire Moors are examples of such attempts at direction. Even earlier than these are the milestones erected during the Roman occupation.

This fingerpost from south Warwickshire was erected as a result of the Turnpike Acts. Boards with destinations were attached to the arms.

The earliest known piece of legislation concerning such signage was passed in 1697 and permitted magistrates to erect signs at crossroads to indicate the route. Then followed the General Turnpike Act of 1773, by which the trustees of various schemes were required to erect suitable signs informing travellers of the distance to the nearest towns, and often also to London. There are still in existence many milestones and a few fingerposts dating back to this period. The earliest known fingerpost is 'Joseph Izod's Post', which stands on the A44 in the high Cotswolds and is dated 1669. There are even a few warning signs that predate the motoring age: on a road skirting Dartmoor there is a stone advising the drivers of horse-drawn coaches to 'take off' some of their horses. This book, however, deals with signs erected to address the traffic requirements arising as a direct consequence of the development first of the bicycle and then of the motor vehicle.

The earliest signs of the present era were installed not by the local authorities, as most are today, but by organisations established specifically to help the cyclist and, later, the motorist. Such organisations included the

Above: *One of the effects of the Turnpike Acts was that the trustees were able to levy charges on travellers. This scale of charges was levied between Kingsteignton and Chudleigh in Devon.*

Left: *This is a replica of Joseph Izod's Post in the Cotswolds. The original is cared for by a local history group. It was removed by the County Council for safe keeping.*

DORSET

ANY PERSON WILFULLY INJURING ANY PART OF THIS COUNTY BRIDGE WILL BE GUILTY OF FELONY AND UPON CONVICTION LIABLE TO BE TRANSPORTED FOR LIFE BY THE COURT

7 & 8 GEO 4 C 30 S 13   T FOOKS

Above: These eighteenth-century bridge signs are still to be found throughout Dorset. Perhaps the same harsh punishment would prevent some of the damage to current signs!

Left: During the eighteenth century, in order to protect the highway, magistrates permitted extra horses to be used only on steep hills. At the summit, these extra horses had to be 'taken off'. This example is still on the roadside south of Okehampton.

Bicycle Union, later known as the National Cyclist Union, and the Cyclists' Touring Club, followed by the Automobile Association (AA), the Royal Automobile Club (RAC) and local motoring clubs. These early signs have now disappeared from the highways and are much sought after by collectors.

Signs erected by the cycling organisations were primarily intended to warn cyclists of two hazards: sharp corners and steep hills. On the steepest hills, a sign depicting the skull and crossbones served as a warning to take extreme care. Another early example of a warning sign is that of the diamond,

The Automobile Association (AA) was one of the motoring organisations that produced signs. Here are four examples of their signs in the familiar yellow with black writing. These were introduced in 1911.

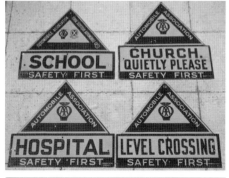

Some of the earliest signs were erected by cycling organisations. This warning was necessary because cycle brakes at the end of the nineteenth century were not as efficient as those of today!

erected, often by railway and canal companies, to advise of the maximum load that a bridge was expected to carry.

By the onset of the twentieth century there was such a proliferation of signs that many no longer served the purpose for which they had been designed. With the likelihood of confusion being caused by all these signs, the Government (there was no Ministry of Transport at that time) stepped in and, through the Motor Car Act of 1903, made legislative provision for local authorities to erect the signs they deemed necessary. It is the development of these signs that this book will now examine.

The local authority signs can be divided into three broad groupings (each of which is dealt with in detail over the following chapters). The first, and probably today the most important, group is that of the warning, mandatory, restriction and prohibition signs erected to contribute to road safety. The second group is that of the direction signs, aiding the traveller in his or her journey by providing instruction on the way to go. These vary from the large motorway signs to the humble fingerpost along a country lane, both serving the same purpose and both equally appropriate to their specific situations. The final group of signs to be dealt with is that of the location signs, which give information – through, for instance, a boundary sign – about where a traveller is situated when observing the sign.

These 'diamond' signs were erected by the railway and canal companies, as a result of the 1896 and 1903 Acts, to protect from damage the bridges they erected to cross their railways or canals.

WARNING, MANDATORY, REGULATORY AND PROHIBITION SIGNS

Three signs authorised following the Motor Car Act of 1903. They are (from left to right): speed limit; general hazard warning; prohibition sign.

Motor Car Act, 1903

After the emancipation of the motor car from the red flag in 1896, the Government enacted the first major piece of legislation on road signs. The signs proposed were for indicating crossroads, steep hills and dangerous corners. Following this Act, in 1904 the Government issued a circular stating that warning signs were to be in the form of a red triangle, although the reason for the caution was not stated on the sign, and prohibition was to be signified by a solid red disc. Some of these early signs can be found in museum collections. There was a general speed limit at the time of 20 mph (32 km/h). Other speed limits were also in force and these were indicated by a white annulus (ring top), beneath which was placed the speed limit on a plate.

Standardisation of Road Direction Posts and Warning Signs, 1921

In 1919 the Ministry of Transport was created to replace the Road Board, which had existed since 1910. One of the first results of the creation of a ministry was the classification of roads. From this date, such classifications as A38 and

A sign from 1903 warning of a dangerous corner was still performing its role in the 1970s on the Isle of Wight.

B6110 began to appear. The system devised took into account many characteristics: national importance of the road, volume of traffic, and so on. (While 'C' roads do exist, they are rarely indicated as such. An example of a 'C' road that *is* indicated can be found on a fingerpost near Holmfirth in Yorkshire.)

The Minister of the day also appointed a committee to examine the use of signs on the highway. The result of these deliberations was the 1921 Memorandum. It is of note that nearly all legislation about road signs has come in the form of either circulars or orders now published as Statutory Instruments. Because of the constantly changing thoughts on signage, Parliament wisely decided to enact enabling legislation. This was of a general nature and left the Minister to determine the detail as conditions demanded. The 1921 Memorandum was a case in point, although it should be noted that all the recommendations contained therein were of an advisory nature only. None the less, most local authorities did adopt its recommendations. At first these were County, County Borough, Borough, Rural District and Urban District Councils, but today Highway Authority means the County Council or its equivalent, such as a Unitary Authority.

It was the 1921 Memorandum that introduced the signs familiar to the older generation, such as the torch indicating a school, or those for a level crossing, corner, double corner, or steep hill. These were to use a symbol on a rectangular plate measuring 12 x 21 inches (30 x 53 cm). Underneath the symbol, lettering was to state the danger that lay ahead. The symbols adopted, with the exception of the school torch, remain in use today, though the form and size may differ slightly from that of 1921.

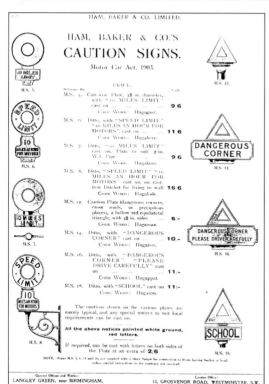

This page from a Ham, Baker & Company catalogue published after 1903 illustrates the variety of 1903 signs available to local authorities. Note the prices!

A 1921 sign still standing in east Devon in 2005. Manufactured by Ham, Baker & Company, it is made of cast iron, which was used alongside enamel for many years.

Memorandum No. 297: Street Traffic Signalling, 1929

In 1926 the first three-aspect (red, amber, green) electric traffic lights were installed in Wolverhampton; the reason for the choice of this town is lost to us. Previous experiments employing hand-operated railway-type signals had not been successful. The Wolverhampton experiment resulted in Memorandum No. 297 being issued in September 1929 to regularise signals of this type. The standard introduced was based on the Wolverhampton model.

Memorandum No. 291 (Roads), 1930

In 1930 the Minister issued this circular advising authorities to erect hazard signs warning of the following: one-way streets, road junctions, level crossings without gates (this sign depicted a 4-6-0 locomotive) and parking places. (The last of these may sound a surprising hazard for 1930, but even at this early date parking had become a problem in some major towns and cities.) Another sign called for in the memorandum was the dead-slow sign. As this had both a warning and a mandatory purpose, it was surmounted by a red triangle within a red circle. An innovation of the time was the introduction of flashing red beacons to warn motorists of important road junctions, particularly at night and in fog.

The Road Traffic Act 1930 gave powers to the Minister to prescribe and secure a uniform system of traffic signs throughout Britain (and was thus an example of enabling legislation). Much of today's traffic-sign legislation arises in a similar way. One of the surprising features of the 1930 act was the abolition of the 20 mph (32 km/h) speed limit for vehicles carrying fewer than seven persons.

The Traffic Signs (Size, Colour and Type) Provisional Regulations, 1933, and resulting changes

The 1933 regulations were enacted

A collection of 12 x 21 inch (30 x 53 cm) signs. Some were commonplace; others, like 'tram pinch', were rarities.

9

NARROW BRIDGE HUMP BRIDGE

TURN LEFT
←
ONE WAY ONLY

Far left: *It was unusual to see signs placed side by side in this way. This photograph was taken at a crossing of the Grand Union Canal in Bedfordshire in the 1970s.*

Left: *Another sign of the 1930s. It is not, however, up to the standard required by the European convention – too many words!*

under the provisions of the Road Traffic Act 1930. There followed a report set up by the Act. This report recommended a series of new signs, which were then legalised by the regulations. The signs thus introduced were for road narrows, narrow bridge, low bridge (any bridge below 16 feet 6 inches – 5.03 metres), roundabout, hospital, no through road, no entry and slow at major road ahead. The symbols were much the same as those used today except that a Maltese cross was used for the hospital sign, and the words 'No Entry' were written across the white band of the sign for that prohibition. Waiting signs were white on blue, enclosed in a red circle. The solid red disc, introduced in 1904, was permitted to have a modifier plate underneath where the prohibition was not total. It was still possible for the AA and RAC to erect standard signs that bore their initials and/or badge as part of the plate. The AA, however, continued to use its own design – much to the annoyance of the Ministry of Transport and the RAC. The 1933 regulations also introduced the black-and-white-banded posts for road signs. Following these regulations, further additions were made to the range of signs.

In 1934 the humpback bridge was introduced, along with the flashing

ROAD JUNCTION

SPEED LIMIT
15
M.P.H.

Far left: *A 1950 regulation sign still doing its job fifty years on. The studs reflected the light and were used before modern reflective materials.*

Left: *Although in the 1930s a general speed limit of 30 mph (48 km/h) was imposed for urban areas, the regulations made provision for lower speed limits to apply where appropriate.*

Right: *The 'halt at major road ahead' sign was shaped in this way to enable motorists to recognise it in the snow. It was more common on highways than today's 'stop' sign.*

Above left: *The interesting point about this 1950s sign is the reuse of a 1903-style post. The initials of County Council of Middlesex can just be discerned on the post.*

Above right: *Authorities were supposed to adhere to designs published in legal documents. Some, however, did produce signs that were unique to their highways, as illustrated by this unauthorised sign near Grosmont, North Yorkshire.*

Right: *Further signs from the collection of 12 x 21 inch (30 x 53 cm) signs dating from 1921 to 1964. In the 1950s aluminium alloy began to replace cast iron in sign construction.*

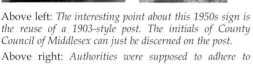

orange globe at pedestrian crossings known as the Belisha beacon (after Hore-Belisha, the Minister of Transport who introduced them). The following year the 'halt at major road ahead' sign was introduced. As a mandatory sign this had the red disc signifying such a requirement, and also the red triangle as a warning of danger. Also in 1935 the 30 mph (48 km/h) speed limit for urban areas was introduced. In 1936 provision was made for cattle and other animals, although these signs did not incorporate the now-familiar silhouette of the animal they warned of. The presence of children was alerted to in another sign, again using the 'torch of knowledge' symbol (for a school).

Report of the Departmental Committee on Traffic Signs 1944, and resulting changes

Although the report is dated 1944, legislation was not enacted until 1950. A

Far left: *This rare sign, by the Crinan Canal, Argyll, is from the 1950 regulations.*

Left: *Another unauthorised sign, this time from the Lake District. Many local authorities erected unauthorised signs such as these, which had no legal standing. Today's authorities are more circumspect.*

recommendation in this report was to invert the triangle in the 'slow at major road ahead' sign (today's equivalent being the 'give way' sign). Presumably this minor change cost the highway authorities a considerable amount in the replacement of outdated, and therefore illegal, signs. This was not the only time such a small change cost a lot of money. The change of typeface for the digit '3' in the 30 mph sign is another example (the top of the '3' being changed from flat to curved).

In 1954 the zebra crossing was introduced for use with the existing orange beacons. The panda and pelican variants of this crossing were introduced in 1962 and 1969 respectively. In 1957, in an attempt to bring UK signs in line with the rest of Europe, the torch symbol on the school sign was replaced by children carrying books, while the 'children playing' sign showed children with a ball. The use of an animal on the 'beware of cattle' sign was also introduced in this year; subsequently, sheep, horses and other animals have been added. It was also in 1957 that regulations were drafted to introduce yellow lines at the kerb of the pavement to denote parking restrictions.

The red 'torch of learning' introduced in the 1921 regulations was replaced by the depiction of children in the 1950 regulations. Satchels date the sign.

An early motorway sign from the Preston Bypass (M6), Britain's first motorway. Like all subsequent motorway signs, it was blue. This was constructed in the now familiar sheet alloy.

Motorway signage – the Anderson Report, 1962

By 1958 the first stretch of motorway, the Preston Bypass (now the M6), was opened in Britain. It was obvious that the signage then in use was unsuitable for these high-speed dual-carriageway roads. Sir Colin Anderson produced a report, published in 1962, that recommended, among other things, the adoption of lower-case letters after the initial capital, and a blue background (the colour already used on Continental motorways). By means of this report, Anderson introduced the motorway signs familiar today. After adoption, the only major addition to the scheme of signs was the inclusion of numbers to indicate the junction. (The sign indicating a motorway, however, was changed once between the interim and final report, and then again subsequently.) The style of motorway signs was a precursor to the next major instigator of change to Britain's road signs – the Worboys Report.

Worboys (1963) and beyond

The 1933 system of road signs had been subject to mounting criticism from the early 1950s. The major concern was that in an age of increasing mobility across national boundaries there should be a system of signs instantly recognisable wherever one found oneself. The reliance on written warnings was not considered sufficient. The adoption of the 1949 protocol would bring the United Kingdom in line with European practice. A committee was then established under Sir Walter Worboys to review the system of road signs, with the exception of motorways (which had already been updated under the Anderson Report). The Worboys Report (as it is universally known) was issued in 1963. It was a radical review of the signage system in use at the time and recommended many changes. It promoted the concept of colour coding routes, the use of lower-case letters and the variation of letter size according to traffic speed (this last recommendation making use of research conducted on drivers' reaction times). As a result of this report, a new

A modern motorway sign familiar to today's motorist. Despite their number, motorway signs are not easy to photograph without risking one's life.

13

alphabet (or typeface) was devised and called, without too much imagination, the Transport Alphabet. The designs of the Worboys committee won a Council of Industrial Design award for graphic design in 1967.

The recommendations were accepted, with minor changes, in the Traffic Sign Regulations of 1964.

The Traffic Signs Regulations and General Directions 1964

Warning signs, instead of being surmounted by the red triangle, now had their symbol contained within the red triangle. The symbols were for the most part those with which the travelling public had become familiar: the cross for crossroads, the gate for level crossings with gates, and so on. There were minor changes, for instance the crossing without gates reverted to the 4-6-0 locomotive (it had been a 0-6-0 since 1950). New signs were introduced, such as those for a tunnel and for overhead cables. Others such as that for a narrow bridge disappeared, 'road narrows' being considered sufficient. The Maltese cross signifying a hospital was also destined for extinction.

Prohibition signs were now to be contained within a red circle, and the familiar 'halt/slow at major road ahead' signs started to be phased out. The blue disc with the instruction in the form of a white symbol (rather than words) was introduced. An example of this is the 'keep left' sign with the white arrow.

Parking signs too were now of the European standard, together with the yellow lines with which those of us who try to park in our congested towns are only too familiar. Incidentally, the guidelines that accompany any regulation detail the parameters of the sign very precisely. The colours, for example, have to be of the British standard specified. The sizes too are precise. Many a motorist has tried, sometimes successfully, to evade conviction from an alleged offence by demonstrating that the sign detailing the prohibition was not of the standard specified in the regulations. Signs must move with the changing needs of the motorist and other road users.

While the basic system introduced by Worboys remains unchanged, there have been many additions and alterations to the particulars.

A steam locomotive is still the symbol authorised by legislation. Such is the popularity of the steam engine that an anachronistic sign is fully understood by today's traveller. From the 1921, 1944 and 1950 regulations.

This drawing accompanied the instructions on revised regulations issued to Cornwall County Council. It illustrates the precise dimensions of road signs. Any departure from these would render the sign unauthorised.

Some significant changes since 1964

Since 1964 the legislation authorising road signs has increased to the extent that Statutory Instruments (the official notification of changes) appear many times a year. The changes detailed often seem insignificant but none the less are important to those who manage Britain's road network.

In 1966 Machynlleth Urban District Council requested permission to use dual-language signs (English and Welsh). Permission was granted in 1967 and in 1985 was extended to all signs in Wales. In the Western Isles the only language used is Gaelic. These are examples of how individual communities, through their local authorities, have influenced the nature of signs to be found on today's roads. This is but one force for change; public opinion can at times be expressed through local MPs, pressure groups or quasi-official organisations (wildlife signs are an example of where such bodies are enlisted to help). Sometimes also the implementation of European legislation is required. Whatever the stimulus, all changes still occur through the enabling legislation published in the Statutory Instruments.

Some further changes to the system include: under 1975 regulations, the replacement of the Worboys 'STOP' sign (a red disc and red triangle with the word 'stop' printed across the face) with the octagonal 'STOP' sign (though the latter is used much less frequently than the former); the introduction in 1977 of the current national speed limits; the installation of the 1981 signs for no footway and elderly people.

While miles are likely to remain as a unit of measurement in signs for some time to come, other metric units, for example those pertaining to height and weight, have been introduced. Since 1983 the height of low bridges has been indicated in both imperial and metric; this was the first example of the now-familiar dual measurement.

An ornate and impressive parish council fingerpost from the banks of the Severn at Ashleworth in Gloucestershire.

DIRECTION SIGNS

Fingerposts

Fingerposts have been around for a very long time. Mention has already been made of Dartmoor crosses and Joseph Izod's Post, of stone and iron construction. However, these are the exceptions to the rule. Most waymarks were made of timber, with directions painted on them, by local people, for local purposes. Those of significance to people living in the area have in most cases been replaced, although occasionally the original name is still attached to the post. The Red Posts found in a number of counties still exist. The function of these remains unclear despite research into the subject. The Red Posts in Devon and Somerset are red in name only. The term 'fingerpost' arises from the use of a stylised finger pointing the way. Although a

Far left: *Not many fingerposts survive in London. This one is lovingly cared for by the local community.*

Left: *This fingerpost is listed because of its literary associations. It appears in the front of Beatrix Potter's 'Pigling Bland'. It is in its original position in Furness in the Lake District.*

This East Lothian County Council direction post demonstrates how the name 'fingerpost' came about. Note, too, the use of unusual fractions of a mile.

widely used term, the first piece of legislation actually to use it was the 1975 circular Roads No. 7/75.

The 1921 Ministry of Transport Memorandum No. 291 provided a model on which direction signs, the official name, should be based. Many authorities adopted this basic model. It was recommended that the name of the authority responsible for the sign's maintenance be included as part of the design. This seemed to inspire county engineers, whose working lives are usually governed by legislation. Perhaps they readily grasped the opportunity to demonstrate their flair, as signs reflecting the individuality of the designer soon began to appear. It seems that each part of the sign – the post, the arms, the method of support, the style of letters, and not forgetting the finial (which was often used to sport the authority's name) – presented the chance for the designers to make their mark. Local pride showed itself in local distinctiveness.

Left: *A sign erected when Rural District Councils were still Highway Authorities. Sadly, these magnificent signs did not remain on the highway for long – they were too popular with vandals.*

Right: *Isle of Ely County Council disappeared in 1965. This post is still maintained in the city of Ely. Authorities vary considerably in their approach to these historical artefacts.*

17

Above left: *Most counties adopted a house style to give their signs distinctiveness, many using an annulus (better known as a 'ring top'). Staffordshire surmounted the difficulty of name length by abbreviation.*

Above centre: *This is an example of how some authorities adapted other authorities' posts that had become their property upon boundary changes. Kemerton, Worcestershire, where this sign still stands, was formerly in Gloucestershire.*

Above right: *Here is a Gloucestershire post to compare with the one from Kemerton. These posts were cast entirely in concrete, with reinforcing bars to prevent serious damage should a motorist hit one.*

It was not until after the Second World War that county councils began to assume full responsibility for fingerpost erection. There are still fingerposts sporting the names of long-since vanished urban and rural district councils, usually with the names painted over. Some have had their finials removed either by the authority or by vandals.

Many counties followed advice to depict the county name, although some, such as Leicestershire, Northumberland and Northamptonshire, did not do so – probably because of the number of letters in the name. Some longer-named counties overcame the problem of length by either abbreviation or use of initials. A selection of other designs can be seen in the accompanying photographs.

The lettering on the signs was usually that of the standard Ministry of Transport design, with a height of 2^1/2 inches (6.35 cm). However, Oxfordshire adopted larger letters for the more important places and smaller ones for those less important. Northamptonshire used letters of 2 inches (5 cm) in height. The variety of designs that county engineers came up with made, and to some extent still makes, a quiet drive around country lanes full of interest. A survey of Devon in 1988 identified forty-two different styles in that county alone.

Far left: A rare survivor this, as Derbyshire thought it had removed all its posts following the 1964 regulations. The incorporation of the date is believed to be unique to Derbyshire.

Left: An example of an authority abolished in 1974. However, first Humberside and now North Lincolnshire have seen fit to retain this sign – albeit with the name painted out!

Below: An Oxfordshire sign illustrating the use of chequers over a route. Varying sizes of letters are used to indicate the differing importance of places. Originally the 'B' route numbers would have been white on black.

Above: Another unique feature was the incorporation of the county crest on Middlesex posts. Again, an example of how successor local authorities care for their heritage.

Left: Another example of local distinctiveness. The use of a 'half-moon finial' was unique to the central parts of Essex. The northern division adopted an annulus and the southern division a disc.

Above left: Do not ever tell a Rutlander that Rutland County disappeared. Small it may be, but full of pride; even the fingerposts are unique to the county.

Above right: The surveyor from the South Hams Division of Devon set himself a challenge as to how many places he could indicate on his posts. This is his masterpiece, now happily preserved at Dingles Steam Village.

All this originality, however, was supposed to come to an end in 1964 with the implementation of the Traffic Sign Regulations recommended by the Worboys committee. Signs were to be of a standard style (although the committee did commend the practice of displaying the county name and recommended its continuance under the new order). Authorities were then issued with instructions to replace their fingerposts. Some complied at once, removing most of their signs. Derbyshire was such a county but, even here, an oversight occurred whereby one lane was missed and there remains a complete suite of pre-Worboys posts from beginning to end. The only former English county authority known to the author with no surviving 'traditional' fingerposts is the Soke of

Far left: A famous, much photographed sign from near Trowbridge, Wiltshire. It indicates the way to two localities in the district – not far away places.

Left: A fingerpost at its most basic. No location, route numbers, finial, miles, or authority responsible for maintenance. Durham County does have more elaborate posts, but this one serves its purpose.

Far left: *Another example of ingenuity from the Nottinghamshire designer. There are still a number in this style to be seen throughout the county.*

Left: *You have to look far and wide to find a traditional post in Surrey. Here is one from near Cranleigh in the south of the county.*

Right: *'M C C' (Merioneth County Council) can still be picked out in black despite that county council having been abolished in 1974. It shares its finial design with Shropshire.*

Peterborough. All others have at least one. Some counties, for example Lancashire, complied half-heartedly with the regulations, resulting in the continuing existence of many fingerposts throughout the county today, while others, including East Sussex, Somerset and Cumberland and its successor Cumbria, just dug in their heels. Somerset posts were manufactured almost one hundred years ago and they are as functional today as the day they were erected.

A graveyard of Devon fingerposts at Torrington. Wooden posts do not last forever. These posts were, shortly after this picture was taken, consigned to the flames.

Left: : *In 1930 the Ministry of Transport asked West Riding and Dorset to include map references on their signs as an experiment. Later, the northern division of Berkshire followed suit.*

Left: *Somerset failed to implement the regulations requiring the removal of pre-Worboys fingerposts; as a result Somerset has one of the most complete sets of traditional fingerposts. This is their smaller-style finial.*

Right: *This sign is from the New Forest in Hampshire. The designer's art is not dead! Unusually for today, this is a cast aluminium sign.*

In 1975 the Department of Transport relaxed the rules to permit the use of the traditional fingerpost in light-trafficked rural roads. This has resulted in the introduction of signs made with newer materials though still to traditional designs.

Advanced direction sign

It soon became apparent, however, that these fingerpost signs were not suitable for the increasing speed of traffic, so in 1930 Memorandum No. 291 (roads) introduced the concept of the advanced direction sign. This enabled traffic to prepare for what lay ahead. Subsequent

Far left: *Like Somerset, East Sussex never adopted the 1964 regulations for its rural fingerposts. The oak posts with the 'black cap' continue to be part of the East Sussex scene.*

Left: *After the 1975 regulations relaxed the rules, some authorities adopted designs made from modern materials. The reader will judge the success of this design…*

A 1933 regulation sign still performing its task three quarters of a century later.

Below: *An advanced direction sign from Scotland. The route to Balmoral should be white on black as for Ballater. A late example of a sign erected by a motoring organisation.*

legislation has refined the styles and information contained within the signs, but the purpose has remained the same. A sign reading 'Fork right Tavistock', for example, prepared the traveller for what lay ahead. However, this sign was limited to giving only a single destination, so in 1933 the map-type advanced direction sign was introduced. These signs had arrows pointing to the direction required; the lettering was black on white, but for the road numbers of 'B' roads white on black was used; and the letters were all to be of a standard height. Another new feature was that roads reached via a main route were indicated by a chequered band above the route number.

The next major change to the system of advance direction signs followed in 1950. This introduced the concept of the local advance direction sign for places in the vicinity. These signs had a white panel containing the directions in black lettering and an arrow pointing the direction, all on a black background. In 1957 black was replaced by yellow as the background colour for through routes, and by blue for local direction signs in urban areas.

The Anderson Report of 1962 (discussed in the previous chapter) heralded a new approach to direction signing. Lower-case lettering of a size

Another advanced direction sign from an earlier age, this time the 1950s, still guiding traffic through Kington in Herefordshire. The background colour of this sign is yellow.

23

A modern sign covering all classifications of roads and much other information besides. The route to Westleigh is bordered in brown, a recent innovation, to indicate a route suitable only for light traffic.

appropriate to the speed of traffic formed the basis of the design.

The 1964 Traffic Sign Regulations (Worboys) introduced the present system of directional signing. The traditional fingerpost was supposed to have been phased out but, in practice, this did not happen on many minor rural roads. None the less, the majority of direction signs were changed to the current pattern following the Worboys Report. Lower-case lettering was used, as were different coloured backgrounds to indicate the class of the road: blue for motorways; green for trunk roads; white for other routes. Local direction signs ended in a point, whereas advanced direction signs had an arrow on a rectangular sign. For a while these signs were white with a blue border, but today they are bordered in black. In the late 1980s local signs with a brown border were introduced to indicate routes suitable for light vehicles only.

BOUNDARY AND OTHER LOCATION SIGNS

The United Kingdom, for convenience of administration, is divided into the territorial units of country, county, region, district and parish. There are other units, often older, that do not perform any administrative function but that are none the less important to the people who live there. Towns and villages today often form part of the larger unit, but one speaks of one's town rather than one's district. Both types of territorial unit are recognised by the legislation that governs traffic signs. The guideline that accompanied the Worboys Report says: 'Signs indicating the name of a town or village and sometimes the name of a place, for example a suburb, within a town interest and assist drivers. This type of sign can also be used at a County Boundary, showing the name of the County.' This guideline also permits the use of a crest and the use of river names. This regulation, of course, merely defines a practice that has been evident on British roads for a long time. Some parish boundary signs predate motorised traffic by many years.

National

To take the largest unit first, the country, there have been signs displayed at national borders for many years. At first they were simply intended to inform the motorist when another country had been

Above: In the eighteenth century, when this sign was made, the parish was the most important unit of local government. Hence it was important to know where your 'patch' ended.

Left: A well-cared-for eighteenth-century sign on the Somerset/Dorset boundary.

Below: The regulations allow points of interest, such as a river, to be indicated to the traveller. This is the River Avon sign at Bradford-on-Avon, complete with the Wiltshire arms.

The Scottish regions were created following the 1974 reorganisation. The latest round of reorganisation, in the 1990s, got rid of Roxburgh – administratively at least!

Left: *An early border sign in Radnorshire. No sign of the Red Dragon anywhere!*

entered. Wales and Scotland tended to display these national signs, whereas in England the county received prominence at the 'frontier'. Nowadays these signs are used as promotional signs. As you leave Scotland at Gretna you are encouraged to return with the words 'Haste ye back'.

County and region

The concept of the county was fairly well understood as a unit until the various changes imposed upon us since 1965 (changes in 1888 at least recognised traditional boundaries). What most people think of as their county may differ from the legal administrative unit bearing the same name.

Before 1950

At first county boundary signs were introduced to aid those responsible for highway maintenance to see where their 'patch' began and ended. The earliest of these county boundary signs predate motorised traffic. They are often wedge-shaped, with the appropriate county name on each face. Some of these signs still remain.

Somerset County Council had signs manufactured and placed on each of the administrative boundaries of the county. So, although Bath at the time (1908) was within the geographical county, it was a separate

Above: *This early boundary sign stood for many years outside the village of Mickleton in Gloucestershire. Sadly, it was stolen in the early 1990s.*

Far left: *Although from 1974 Peterborough was part of Cambridgeshire, it was historically in Northamptonshire. However, the Soke prided itself on its independence and had its own county council.*

Left: *The Chipping Norton Iron Company manufactured this sign. It has since been fully restored and is now a listed monument. This was a very popular design, particularly in the Midlands.*

Above left: *Part of the collection of 1950s boundary signs at Dingles Steam Village. A sign from each traditional English county is represented somewhere in this book.*

Above right: *Scotland has relatively few old signs remaining and so is less well represented in this book. This photograph was taken in 1960 when Ross and Cromarty was still an administrative county.*

Left: *Like Scotland, Wales has fewer old signs remaining. This pre-1974 boundary sign is dated because it is in English only.*

Right: *Northumberland uses its boundary signs to proclaim a message. Presumably Cumbria or any of the counties bordering Wales could carry the same message!*

county borough. Many of these signs are still *in situ*, serving their original purpose after nearly a century. (They are too small for safe observation by the modern motorist.)

A modification of this type of sign was manufactured by the Chipping Norton Iron Company, which placed the legend in an oval at the top with the county names on the face. One or two of these survive, jealously guarded by their counties as listed historic monuments.

After 1950

The English, particularly, have always taken great pride in their counties. It was natural, therefore, that each county should erect signs at its boundary indicating to the passing motorist that Anyshire had now been entered. These began to appear in the 1950s and, for the most part, were cast alloy bearing the name of the county and its armorial bearing (usually known as the coat of arms or crest). All English counties adopted such signs, with the exception of the County of London. Shetland, having no land boundary with the rest of Scotland, erected a sign at the point of entry to the islands in Lerwick.

By the late 1970s it became apparent to the authorities that a county logo rather than a complicated coat of arms, which not many people recognised, would be more appropriate in the days

Being an insular county, the Isle of Wight has a great deal of county pride – hence the sign at the port of entry. It is also an example of a sign mentioning twinning.

A 1950s sign that survived two reorganisations of Cambridgeshire, hence the pre-1965 crest. This is from the border with Suffolk.

Is this a boundary sign or a statement of nationhood?

of image consciousness. Lancashire – the Red Rose County – is one example. And Cornwall, recognising its Celtic distinctiveness, adds 'Kernow' (Cornish for 'Cornwall') to its signs, both old and new. Devon bucks this trend in that, with the loss of Plymouth from the administrative county, the recognisable logo of Drake's *Golden Hind* has been replaced by its coat of arms.

Most county boundary signs are today manufactured from modern materials, such as sheet alloy, with screen-printed lettering; often the sign is presented in bright colours.

Before major changes occurred in 1974, the question of where to place the sign presented little problem. Even though Birmingham was both a city and a county borough, Warwickshire County Council did not place a boundary sign at the junction of the two authorities because it was recognised that Birmingham, while not in the administrative county, remained in the geographical county. Boundary signs can be a source of irritation to those who feel offended by the changes imposed in 1974. Many people feel that administrative convenience does not reflect local pride. Leicestershire County Council found it impossible to keeps signs at the Rutland boundary during their administration of Rutland from 1974 to 1997. Similarly, Birmingham City Council had its staff on the streets removing West Midlands signs the day the West Midlands County Council was abolished in 1986. On the other hand, Middlesex, which disappeared administratively in 1965, still displays the extinct Middlesex County Council coat of arms at many of its boundaries.

Right: *An example of county pride overcoming bureaucracy. Middlesex County Council no longer exists and the coat of arms died with it. This technicality does not bother the burghers of Hillingdon!*

Below: *In 1997 when Humberside was dissolved, the highways authority made a presentation to the author (third from left) of one of its boundary signs.*

28

Right: *Village signs of this type were authorised in the 1921 memorandum. They are still to be found in Norfolk and Lancashire.*

Above: *This Huntingdonshire District Council sign is identical to that which the former county of Huntingdonshire erected except for the addition of 'District Council'.*

Right: *AA village signs such as this example once adorned most villages in Britain. Some are still in use, but for security reasons this one is from a collection.*

The 1990s and beyond

The boundaries of the newly created unitary authorities are clear, even if they do not always meet local pride and aspirations. On the A36 south of Bath the highway passes from Bath and North East Somerset (formerly Avon) into Somerset. The disappearance of Avon was welcomed by nearly all the inhabitants of North Somerset as a return to the county to which they always felt they belonged. Somerset County Council used to maintain a sign at the border between Somerset and Avon; since the creation of Bath and North East Somerset it has disappeared – either officially or by the hand of someone wishing to demonstrate that Somerset had been reached long before that point. Even the humble road sign can be a cause of political unrest!

Towns and villages

What has been said of counties applies also to cities, towns and villages. Many towns lost their civic status in 1974, and so one often sees signs stating the name of the 'ancient' or 'former' borough of the town. Huntingdonshire is now a district and as such it displays a sign with its name at its boundary. Cambridgeshire, the county in which Huntingdonshire resides for administrative purposes, insisted, however,

This is a sign placed at the entrance to a place that is not an administrative unit. It also combines the use of brown tourist signs with a reference to twin towns.

Above left: *The only modern sign known to the author containing the word 'hamlet'. This is Ford Street, below the Blackdown Hills in Somerset.*

Above right: *This sign, found at the entry point to Luton, contained three pieces of information: how far to the next major town; where you have just arrived; and how far you have come. It is a sign typical of the 1950s and 1960s.*

Left: *A village sign erected by the Somerset administrative county. This sign stands on the border with Wiltshire. After a period in Avon, Freshford is now back in Somerset.*

Below left: *A 1950s version of a village sign in Kent, complete with county crest. The county owned the village name-plate and the village the county arms!*

Below right: *A modern version of Kent village signs, manufactured in silk-screen printing on sheet alloy.*

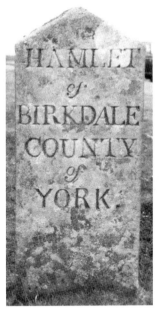

Above: *In 1951 the Festival of Britain was held as a 'tonic for the nation'. Bedfordshire commemorated the occasion with these tasteful village signs.*

Near right: *Situated high up in the Pennines, the boundary stone could be entitled 'little and large' as it demarcates the smallest settlement, a hamlet, and the largest county, Yorkshire.*

Far right: *This parish boundary stone was erected as part of the millennium celebrations in the author's parish, showing that local community pride does still survive in modern society.*

that the words 'district council' be added to avoid the misunderstanding that Huntingdonshire was a county.

Many villages now incorporate the county logo as part of their design (the requirement that they be black on white has been relaxed). Kent and East Sussex adopted such a design when village name plates used to be manufactured out of cast alloy in the 1950s. Humberside did so before its demise, and Northamptonshire and the revived Worcestershire still do so. A variant of this pattern is in Bedfordshire, where the village names incorporate the 1951 Festival of Britain logo.

Parishes

Although parishes are denoted by boundary signs, many of these signs are too small for the motorist to see. This is a pity, as parishes represent the oldest administrative units in Britain.

A joint parish and county boundary sign, complete with arrows to avoid confusion.

31

FURTHER READING

All the books and booklets listed below are published by HMSO (London) but most are now available only in libraries and record offices.

Department of the Environment *et al. Circular ROADS No. 7/75 Size, Design, and Mounting of Traffic Signs.* 1975.

Department of Transport. *The History of Traffic Signs.* 1991. A good general summary; still in print 2001.

Department of Transport, Local Government and the Regions. *The Highway Code.* 1999; still in print. (First edition 1931.)

Local Government Board. *Circular 10 March 1904 (Motor Car Use and Construction).* 1904.

Ministry of Transport. *Standardisation of Road Direction Posts and Warning Signs.* 1921.

Ministry of Transport. *Memorandum No. 297: Street Traffic Signalling.* 1929.

Ministry of Transport. *Memorandum No. 291: Recommendations for the standardisation of road direction posts, warning signs and traffic notices.* 1930.

Ministry of Transport. *Report of the Departmental Committee on Traffic Signs* (The Maybury Report). 1933.

Ministry of Transport. *Report of the Departmental Committee on Traffic Signs 1944.* 1946.

Ministry of Transport. *The Traffic Signs (Size, Colour and Type) Regulations.* S.1. 1950 No. 953. 1950.

Ministry of Transport. *The Traffic Signs Regulations and General Directions.* S.1. 1957 No. 13. 1957.

Ministry of Transport. *Traffic Signs for Motorways* (Anderson Report): Interim Report 1958; Final Report 1962.

Ministry of Transport. *Traffic Signs* (The Worboys Report). 1963.

Ministry of Transport. *The Traffic Signs Regulations and General Directions.* S.1. 1964 No. 1857. 1964.

Ministry of Transport, Scottish Development Department. *Informatory Signs for use on all-purpose Roads.* 1964.

PLACES TO VISIT

Most local and motor museums display a few signs. The most comprehensive display is at:
Dingles Steam Village, Milford, Lifton, Devon PL16 0AT. Telephone: 01566 783425. Website: www.dinglesteam.co.uk

Among the larger collections are:
Beamish – North of England Open Air Museum, Stanley, County Durham DH9 0RG. Telephone: 0191 370 4000. Website: www.beamish.org.uk

Cotswold Motoring Museum, The Old Mill, Sherborne Street, Bourton-on-the-Water, Gloucestershire GL54 2BY. Telephone: 01451 821255. Website: www.cotswold-motor-museum.com

Milestones: Hampshire's Living History Museum, Leisure Park, Churchill Way West, Basingstoke RG21 6YR. Telephone: 01256 477766. Website: www.milestones-museum.com (The AA's collection of artefacts is on display here.)

National Motor Museum, John Montague Building, Beaulieu, Brockenhurst, Hampshire SO42 7ZN. Telephone: 01590 612345. Website: www.beaulieu.co.uk

The Milestone Society, which is dedicated to recording and preserving all highway signs, can be contacted through: Secretary, Terry Keegan, The Oxleys, Tenbury Road, Clows Top, Kidderminster, Worcestershire DY14 9HE. Website: www.milestone-society.co.uk

The feet probably make this an unauthorised sign! It is from rural Kent. Badgers in Shetland and toads in Gloucestershire are other examples of animal welfare signs.